Hi there fellow color enthisiasts!

If you're enjoying this coloring book we'd love to hear your thoughts!

Leaving a review is super easy and only takes a minute, but it means the world to us. Your feedback helps us make more amazing designs for you to color and share with friends.

Thank you

© Rory McGinlay Coloring Books 2023

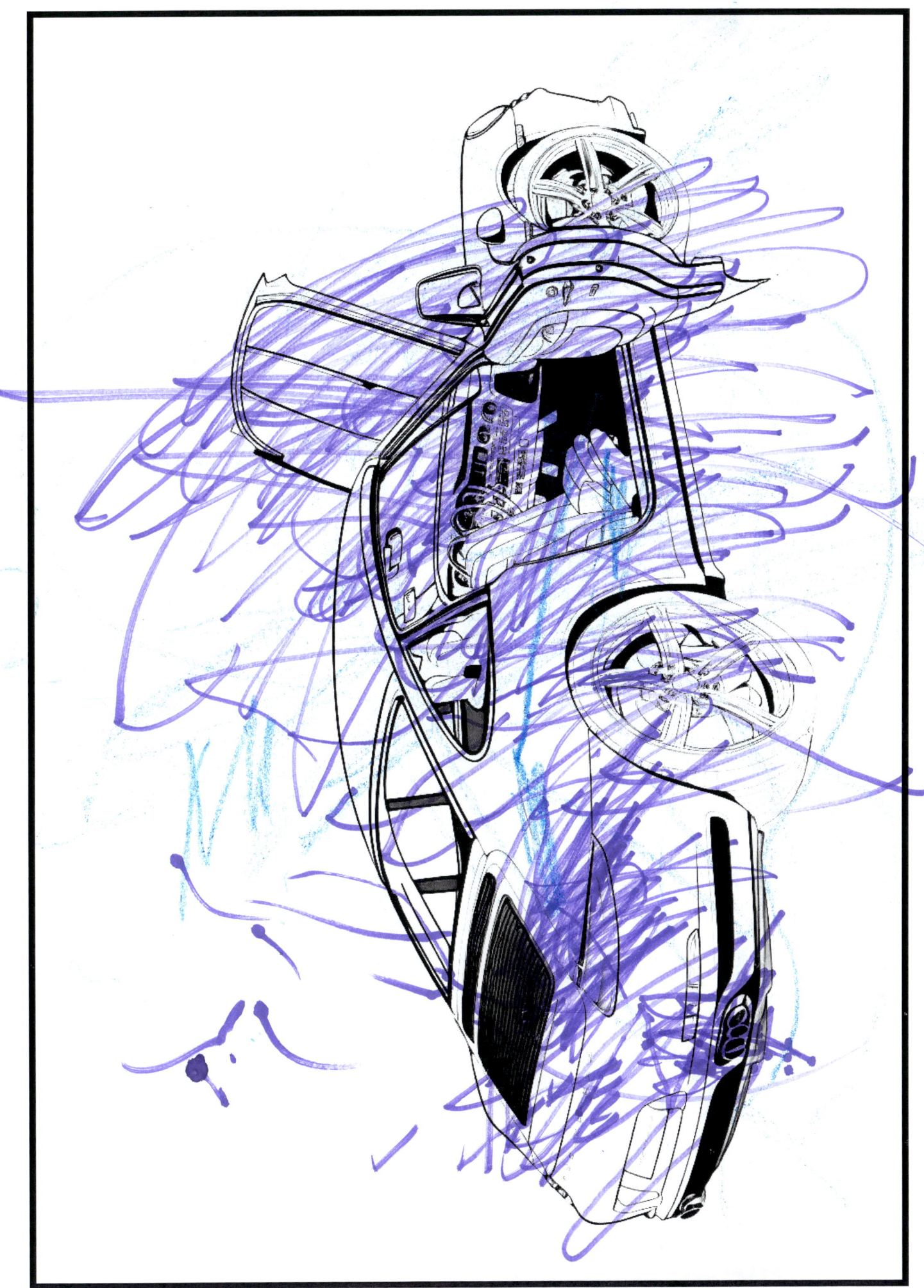

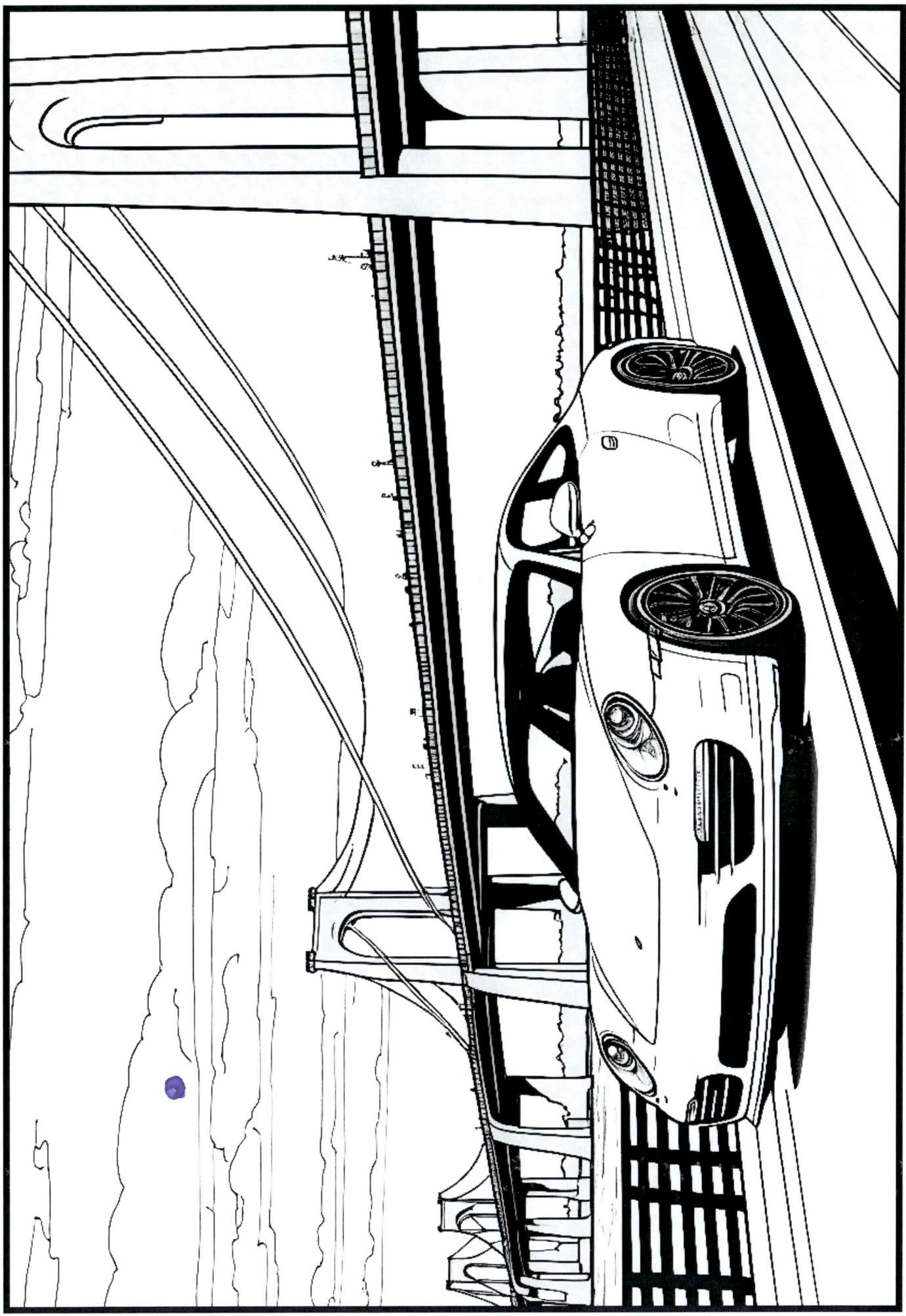

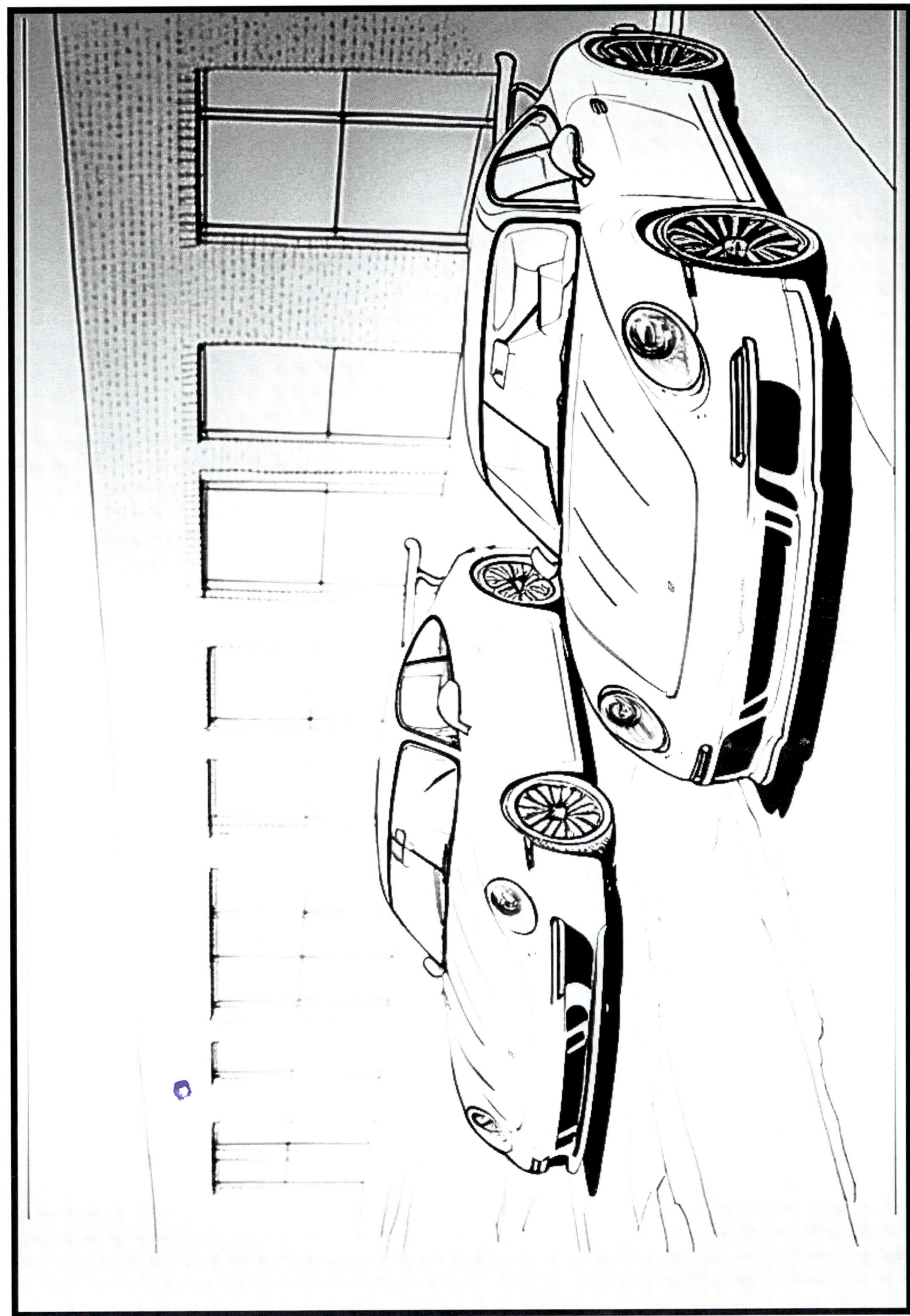

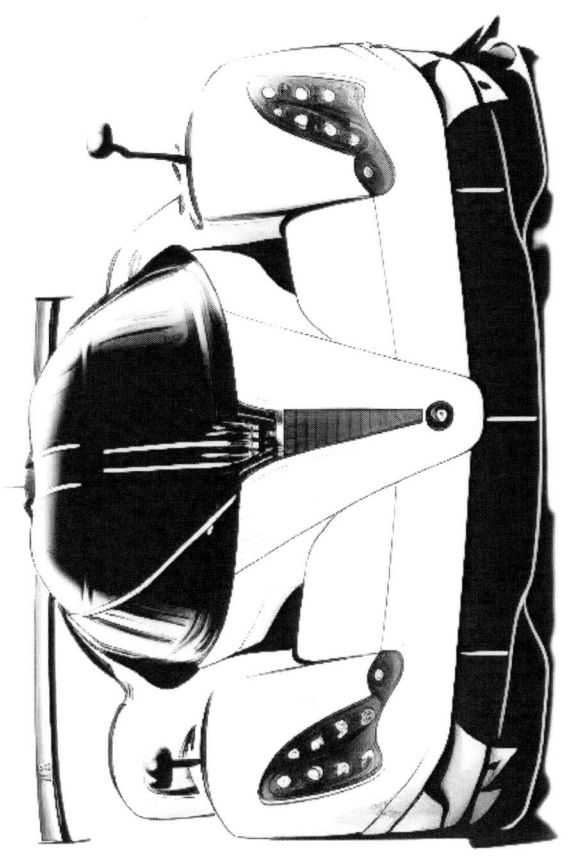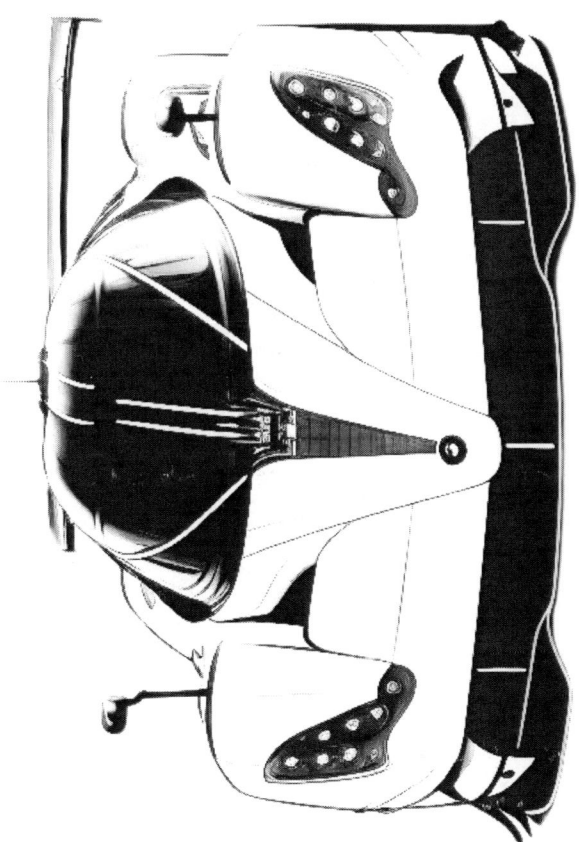

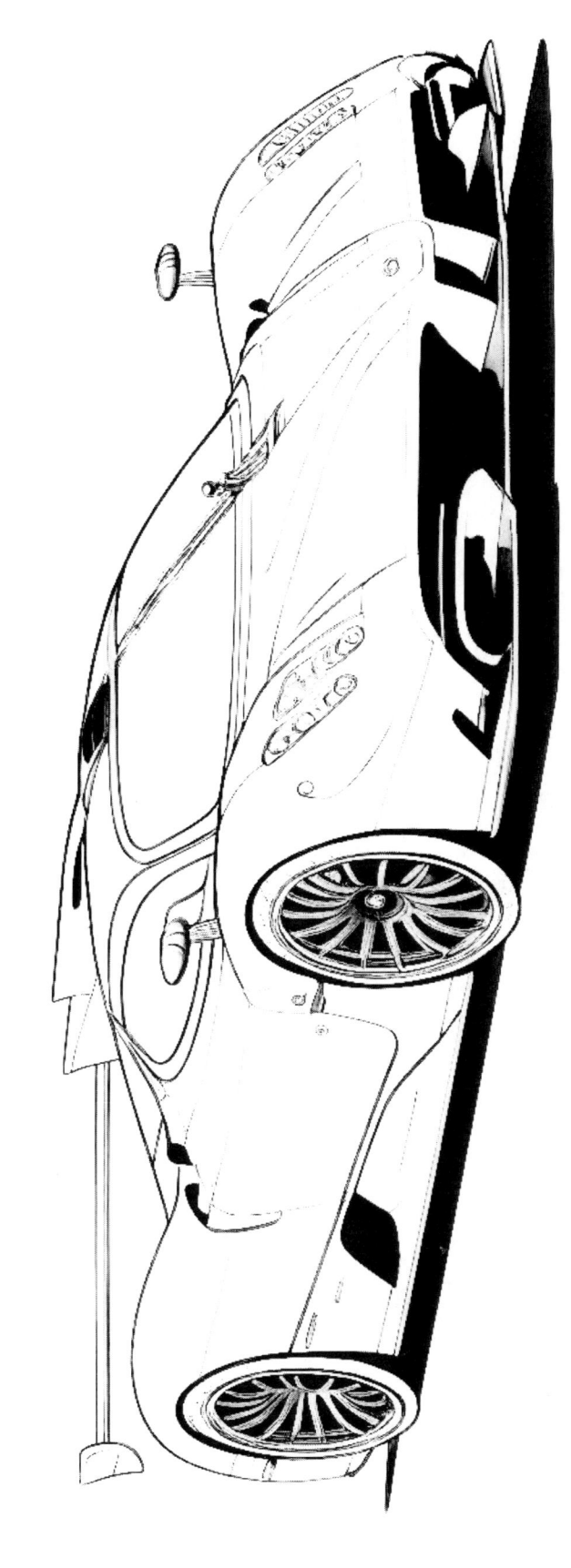

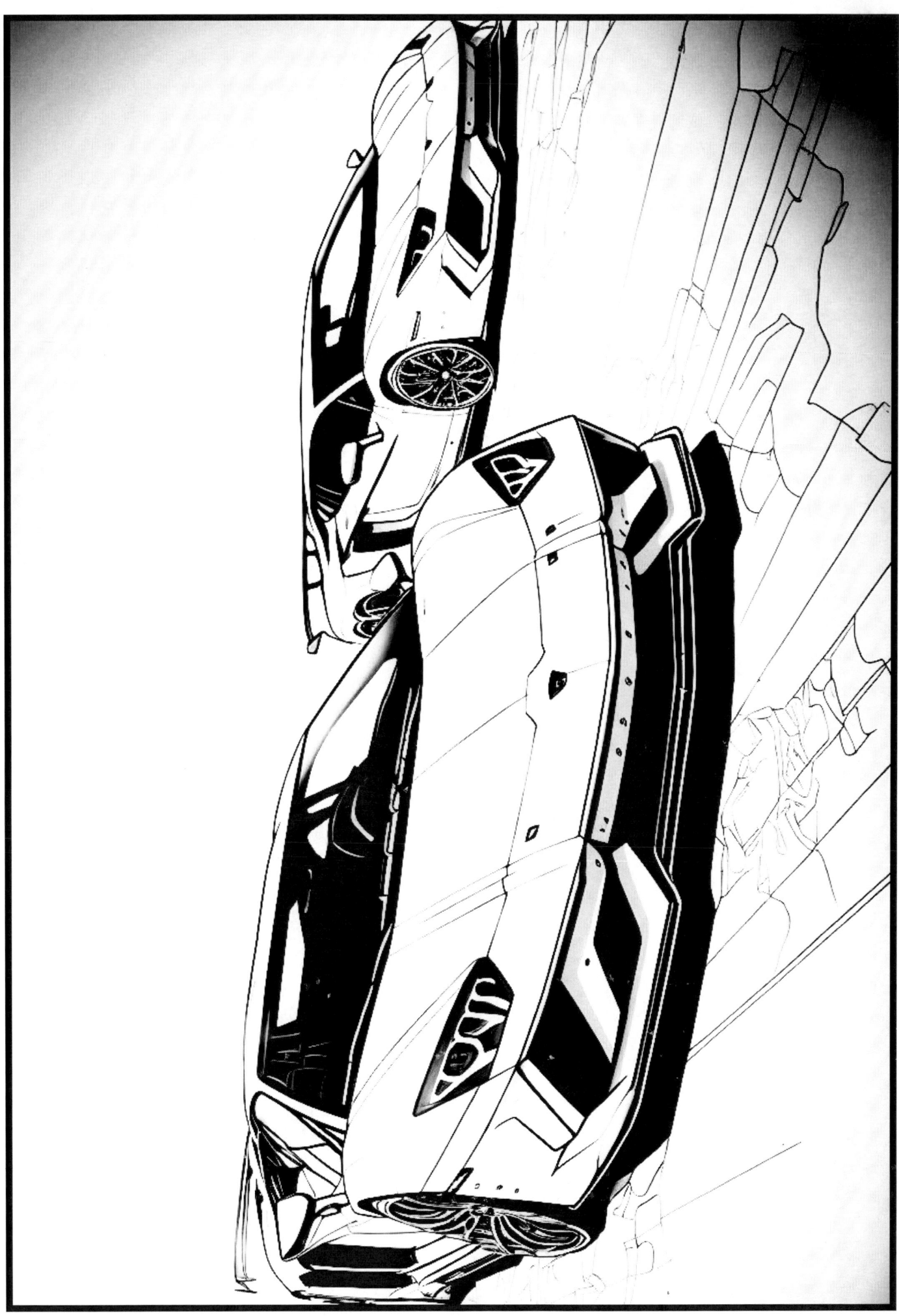

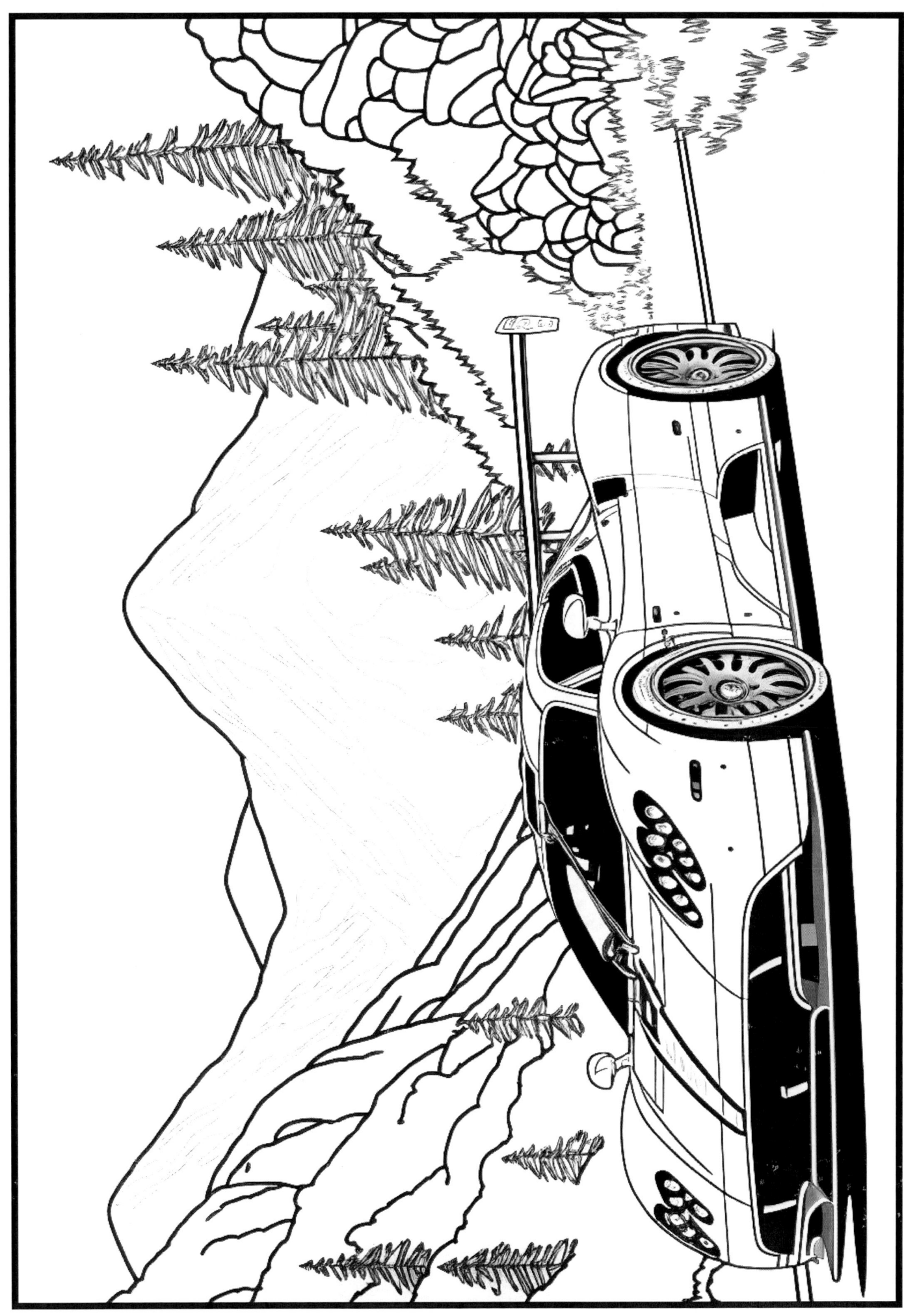

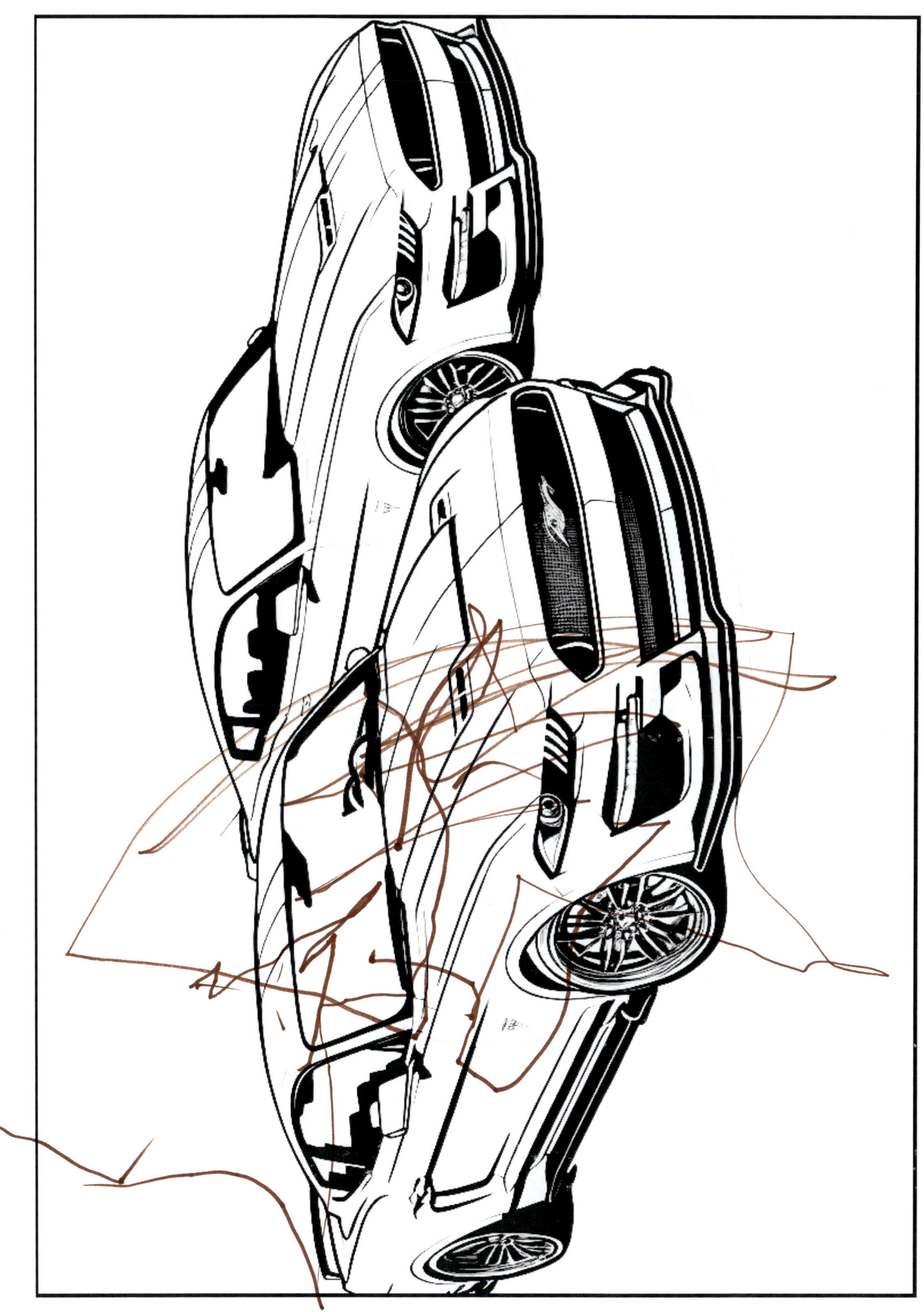

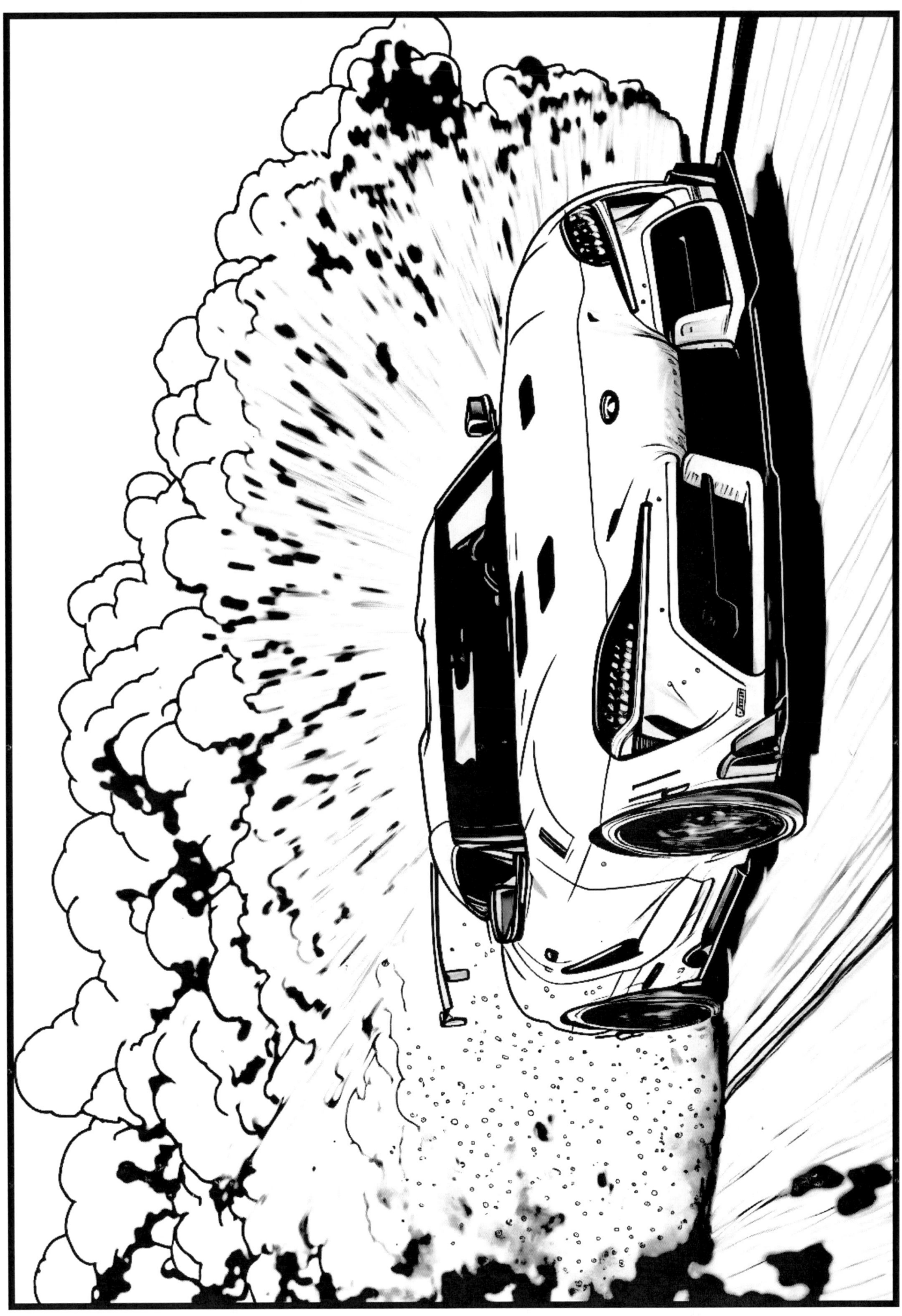

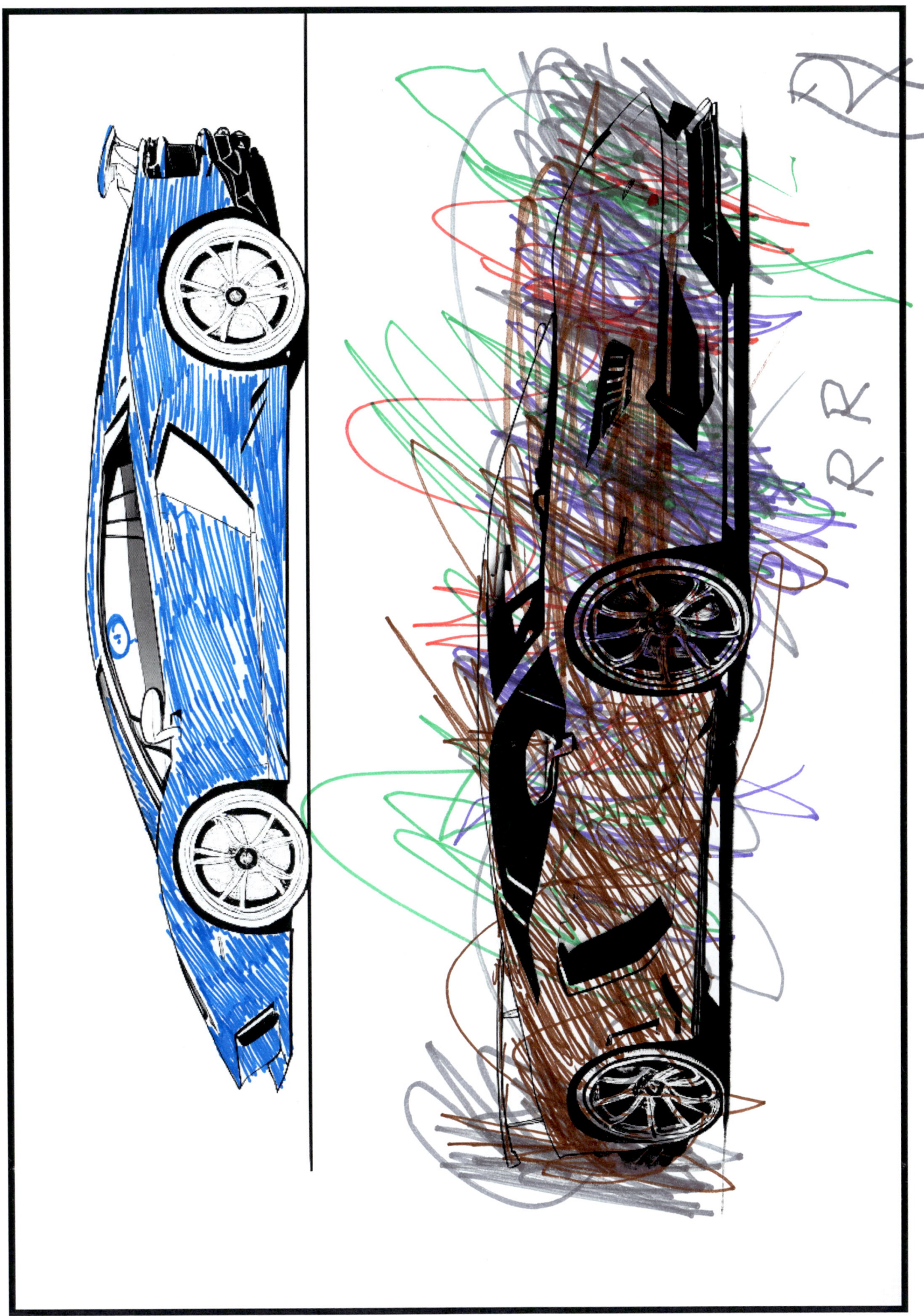

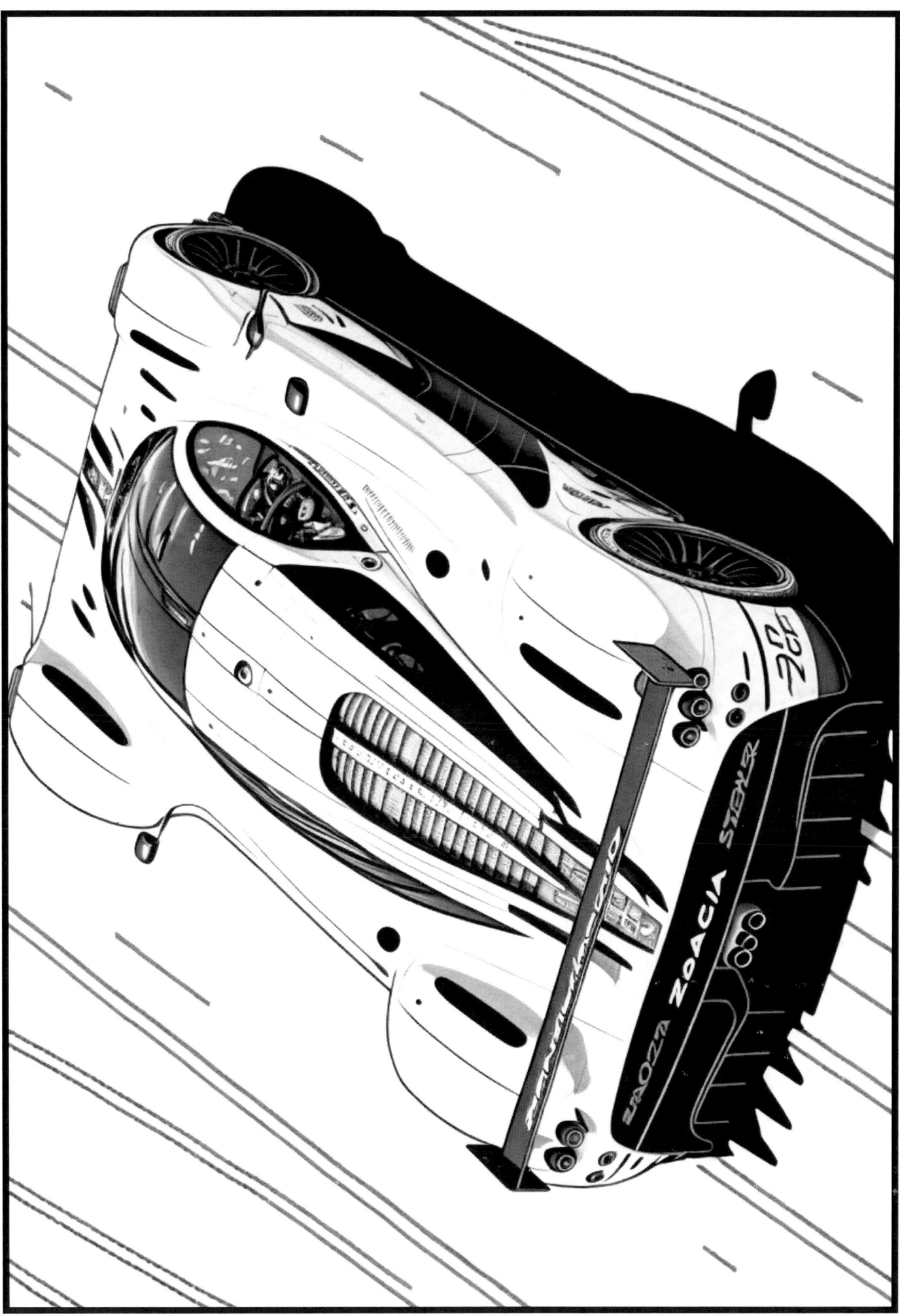

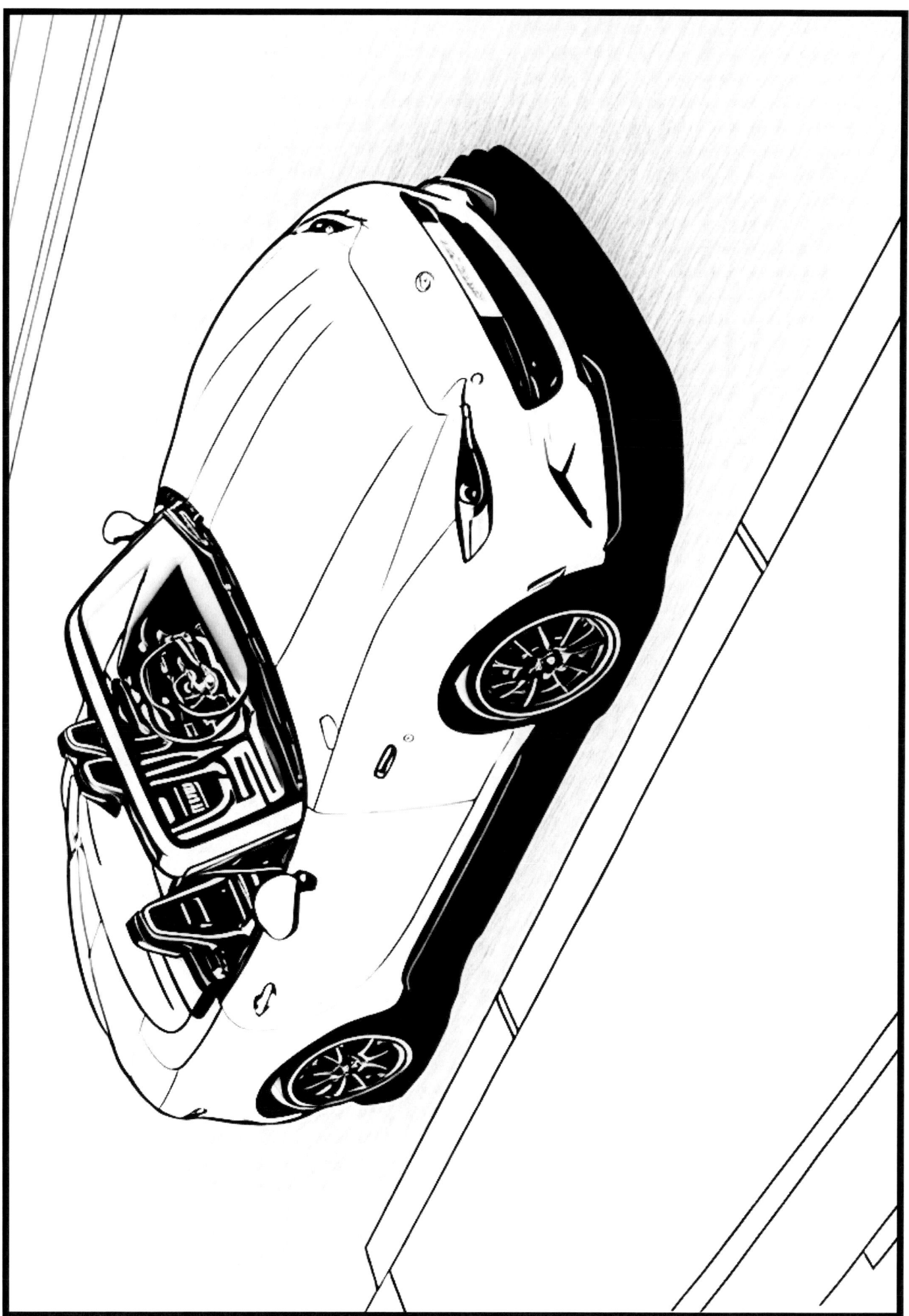

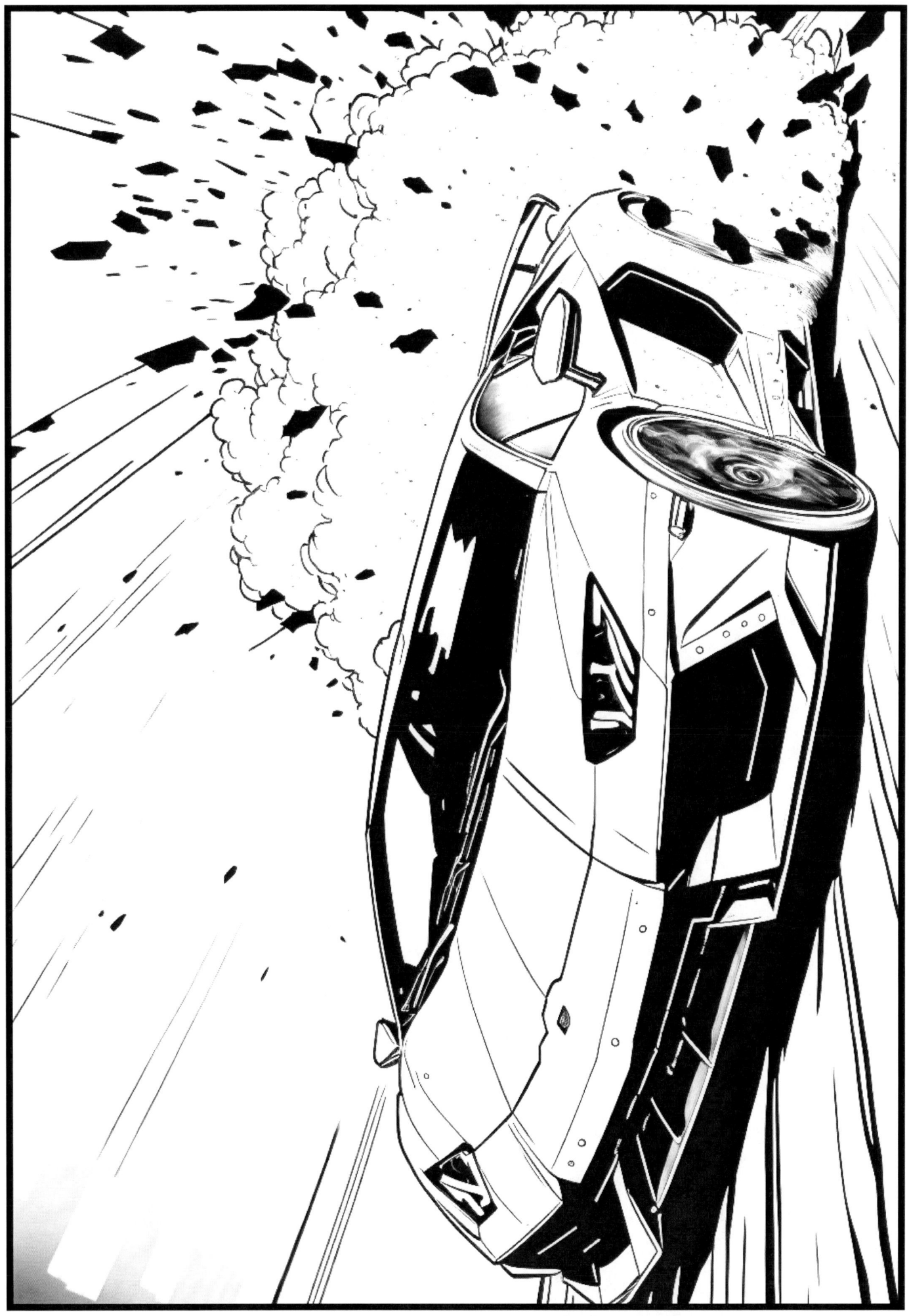

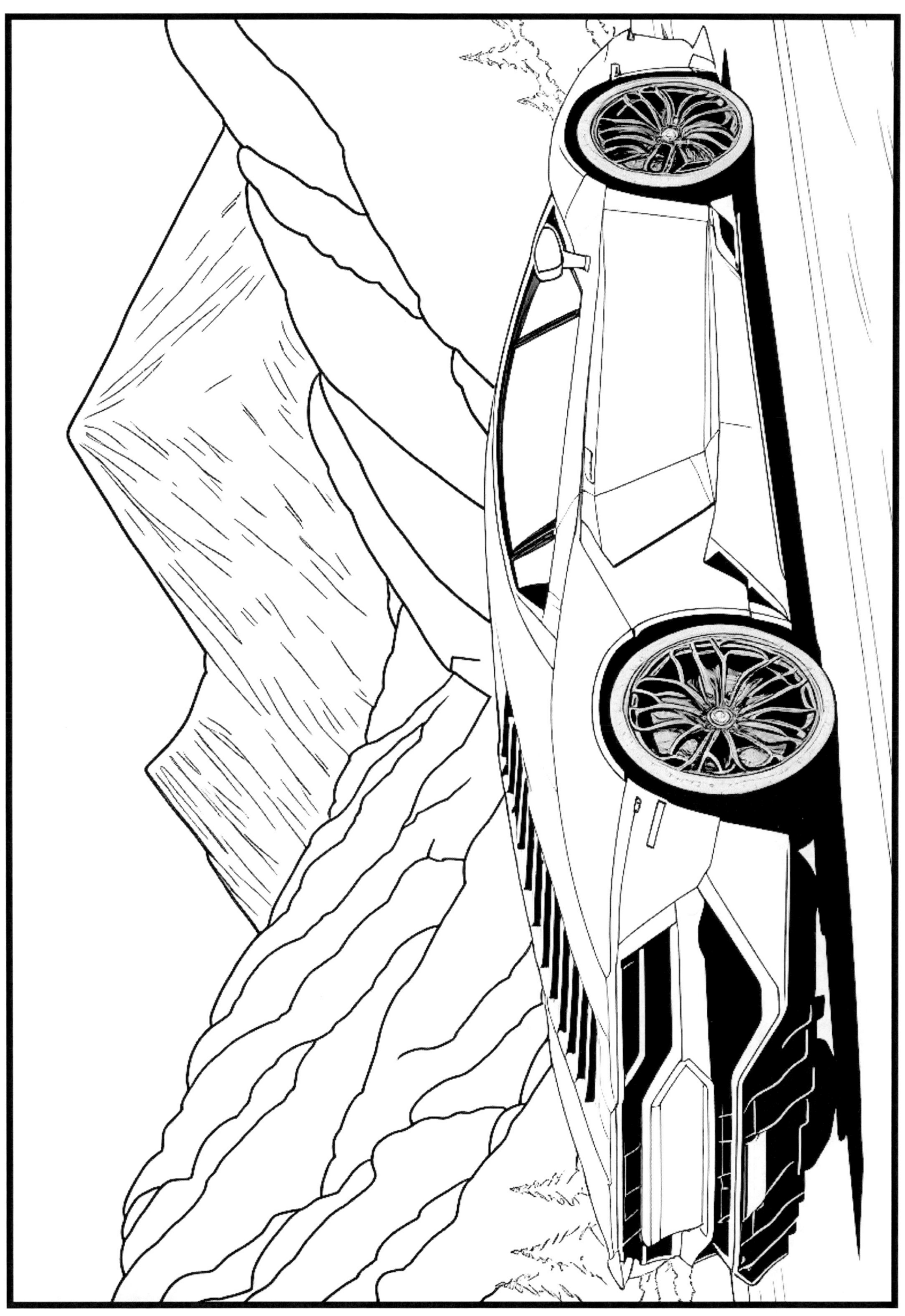

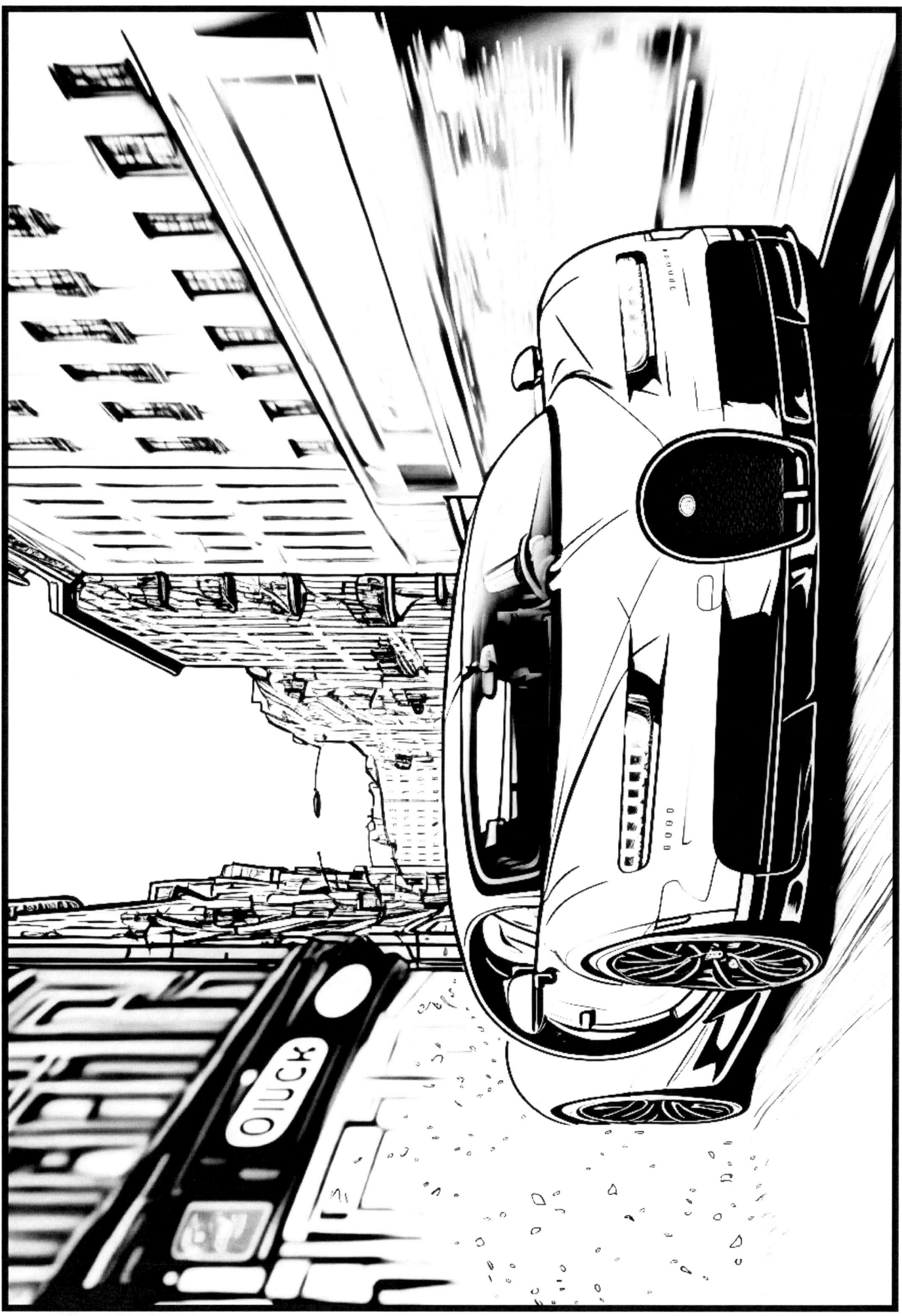

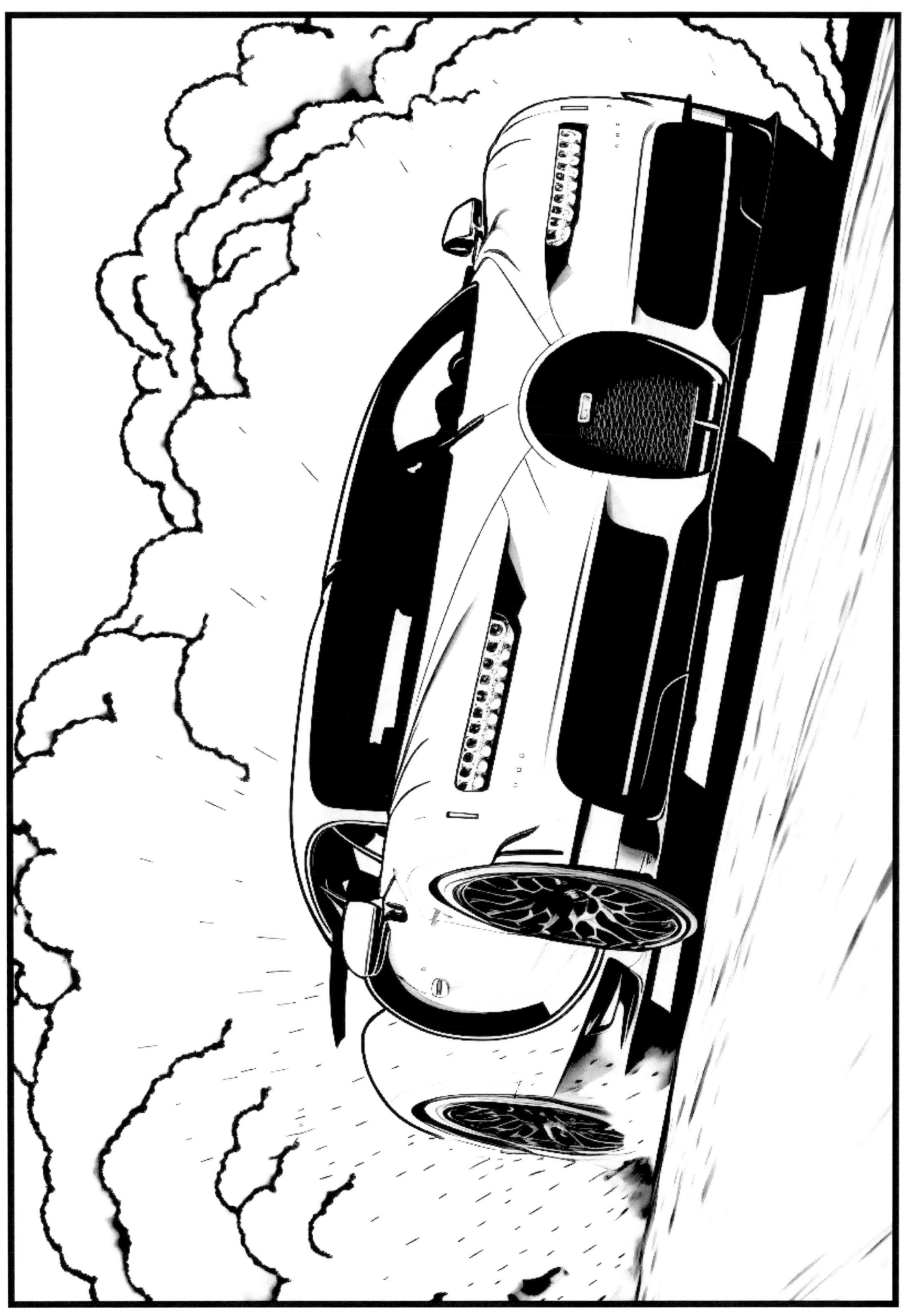

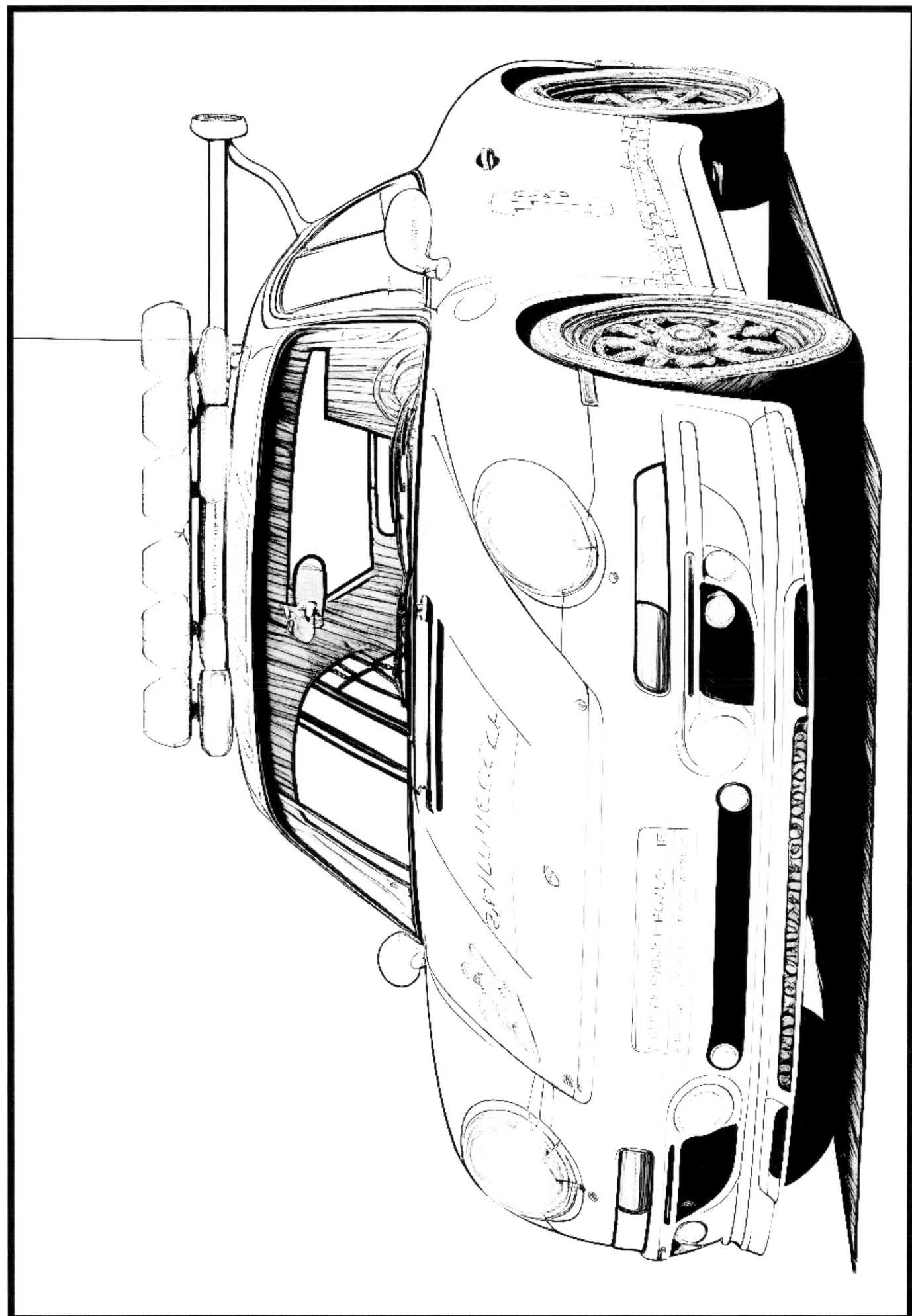

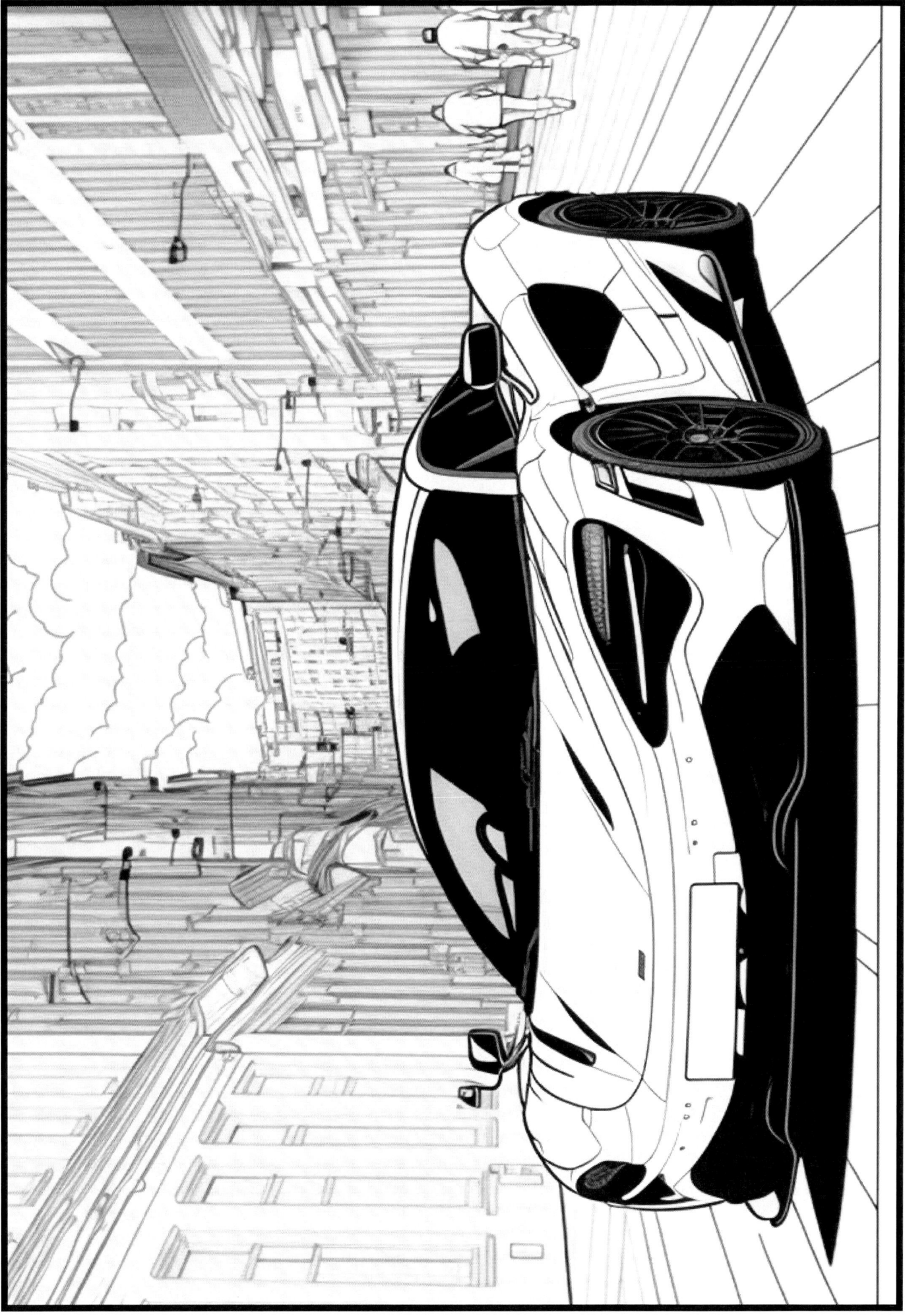

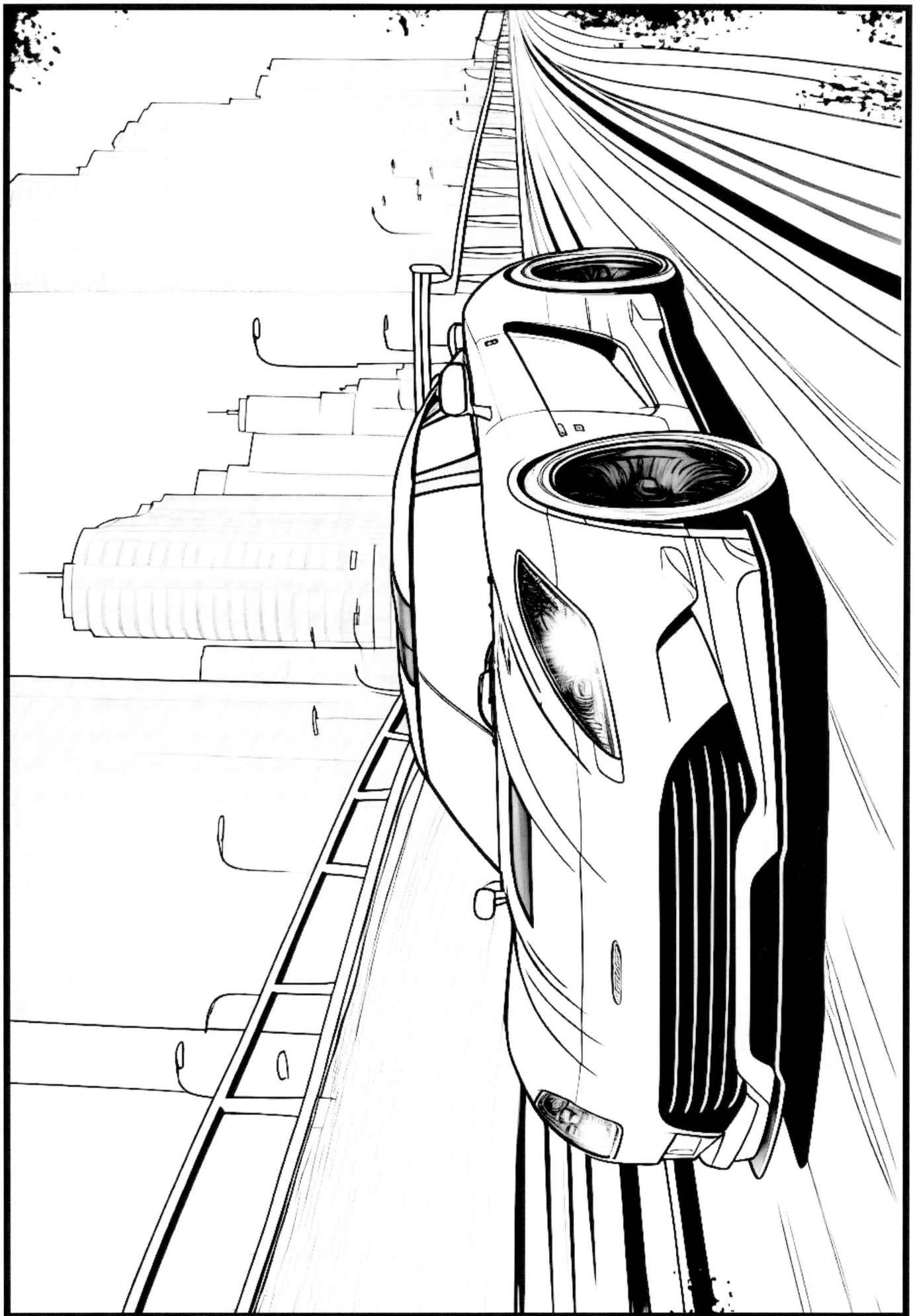

Manufactured by Amazon.ca
Acheson, AB